HILLSBORO PUBLIC LIBRARIES
Hillsboro, OR
Member of Washington County
COOPERATIVE LIBRARY SERVICES

BIOMES
of the World™

OCEANS
Underwater Worlds

Simone Payment

HILLSBORO PUBLIC LIBRARIES
Hillsboro, OR
Member of Washington County
COOPERATIVE LIBRARY SERVICES

rosen publishing's
rosen
central®

New York

Published in 2009 by The Rosen Publishing Group, Inc.
29 East 21st Street, New York, NY 10010

Copyright © 2009 by The Rosen Publishing Group, Inc.

First Edition

All rights reserved. No part of this book may be reproduced in any form
without permission in writing from the publisher, except by a reviewer.

Library of Congress Cataloging-in-Publication Data

Payment, Simone.
Oceans: underwater worlds / Simone Payment.
    p. cm.—(Biomes of the world)
Includes bibliographical references.
ISBN-13: 978-1-4358-5004-0 (library binding) 39531776   2/09
ISBN-13: 978-1-4358-5430-7 (pbk)
ISBN-13: 978-1-4358-5436-9 (6 pack)
1. Marine biology. 2. Ocean. I. Title.
QH91.P37 2009
577.7—dc22

                                          2008023716

Manufactured in the United States of America

On the cover: A school of fish swim around a coral reef.

CONTENTS

INTRODUCTION

The earth's oceans are huge and full of thousands of types of plants and animals. Although we know a lot about oceans, they are also mysterious. Because they are so deep and enormous, 90 percent of the world's oceans have not yet been explored. There may be many types of plant and animal life that we haven't encountered.

In studying the earth, you could look at the globe as land versus water. You could further divide the land into continents, countries, or states.

One convenient way to study the earth is to group areas that have similar climates and plants. These areas are called biomes. You're probably already familiar with the idea of biomes, even if you've never heard the word before. Deserts, forests, and oceans are all examples of biomes.

You could divide biomes into two loose categories: terrestrial (land) and water. Breaking it down even further, terrestrial biomes can be separated into many categories: tropical rain forest, coniferous forest, desert, and many others. Terrestrial biomes are grouped based

Sea turtles live in every ocean around the world except the Arctic. To breed, some green sea turtles travel up to 1,300 miles (2,100 kilometers) between their feeding ground and where they lay their eggs. They use the earth's magnetic field to navigate their journey.

on plants that are most common in those regions and how those plants adapt to the climates.

It is not as easy to divide the water biomes based on plant life and climate. This is because the climate and plant life in a body of water is more uniform than it is on land. Instead, there are two main water biomes: freshwater and ocean. This book will cover some of the many fascinating things about the ocean biome.

CHAPTER 1

OCEANS: THE LARGEST BIOME

Oceans are by far the largest biome. The five oceans cover 71 percent of the earth's surface. If we take into account the depth of the oceans, then they make up even more of our planet—about 90 percent. That means that the number of people on the planet (currently more than 6.5 billion) live on just 10 percent of the available surface.

The oceans are actually just one enormous body of water. However, geographers divide the water into five separate oceans: Arctic, Atlantic, Indian, Pacific, and Southern (or Antarctic).

The Pacific Ocean is the largest. It covers about one-third (32 percent) of the earth's surface. It is so big that it is larger than all of the land areas of the earth put together. The Pacific is also the deepest ocean, reaching depths of 35,000 feet (10,668 meters) or more in some places. The Pacific Ocean stretches from the Arctic Ocean in the north to the Southern Ocean, and from the east coasts of Asia and Australia to the west coasts of North and South America.

Next largest is the Atlantic Ocean, covering about 20 percent of the earth. Half the size of the Pacific Ocean, the Atlantic Ocean covers the area between the east coasts of North and South America and the west coasts of Europe and Africa. It stretches from the Arctic to the Southern Ocean. The Atlantic

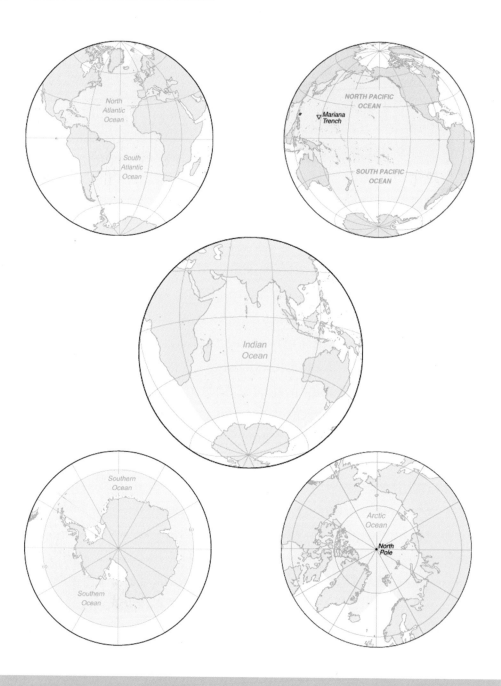

The world's oceans are really just one continuous body of water, covering 139.5 million square miles (about 361.3 million square kilometers).

is approximately 26,000 feet (7,925 m) deep in some places.

The Indian Ocean is similar in size and depth to the Atlantic Ocean. The Indian Ocean is bordered by southern Asia on the north and the Southern Ocean to the south. Africa forms the western border, and Indochina and Australia make up its eastern border.

Two oceans cover the earth's poles. They are the smallest and shallowest oceans. The Arctic Ocean covers the area around the North Pole, reaching down to the northern borders of Asia, Europe, and North America. Much of the Arctic Ocean is sea ice, although in the southern areas of the Arctic, the ice melts during warmer months.

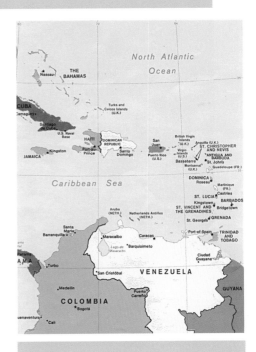

The Caribbean Sea, one of the largest saltwater seas, covers more than one million square miles.

The Southern Ocean, also called the Antarctic Ocean, surrounds Antarctica at the South Pole. Before the year 2000, the Southern Ocean was not officially recognized as a separate ocean. Now, it is considered by most geographers to be the world's fifth ocean. It stretches from the borders of Antarctica to an artificial line (60° S latitude), rather than to another landmass. So, the waters of the Southern Ocean meet the southern areas of the Atlantic and Pacific oceans.

In addition to the five oceans, there are many smaller areas of seawater partially surrounded by land (such as peninsulas or islands). These are called seas and are considered part of the oceans. For example, the Caribbean and Mediterranean seas are both part of the Atlantic Ocean. The Sea of Japan is part of the Pacific Ocean,

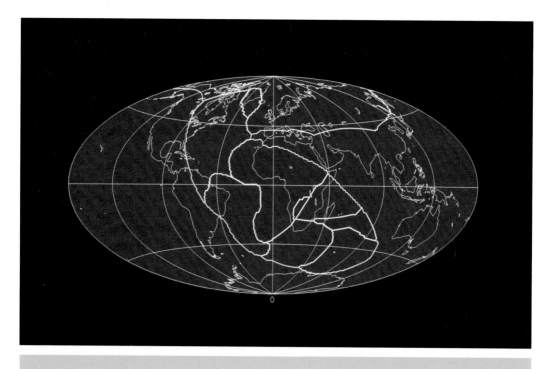

This computer model shows what the continent Pangaea and Panthalassa, the surrounding ocean, might have looked like more than 180 million years ago.

the Red Sea is in the Indian Ocean, and Hudson Bay is part of the Arctic Ocean.

How the Oceans Formed

When the earth formed—about 4.5 billion years ago—it was made up of extremely hot molten rock. Eventually, the outer layer of the molten rock began to cool. As it did, steam escaping from the hotter rock below made rain. Over a long period of time, the rain filled the lower areas of the cooling rock, forming the oceans. Some scientists believe that comets made up of rock and ice hit the earth. This ice contributed to the formation of the oceans when it melted.

THE BOTTOM OF THE OCEAN

The crust is the outer layer of rock covering the earth's core. The oceanic crust lies beneath the ocean floor. It is 4 to 7 miles (6 to 11 kilometers) thick. The crust that forms the continents is thicker. This is why continents are higher than the oceans. Continental crust is 20 to 25 miles (30 to 40 km) thick.

Covering the oceanic crust is sediment. Sediment is made up of many things. Some of it is land that has washed into the oceans from rivers. Some comes from dead plants and animals. The rest is particles that settle out of the seawater. How much of each of these substances is present depends on where they are in the ocean. Areas near the shoreline have more land sediment, for example.

Initially, the ocean surrounded one huge landmass. This ancient landmass is referred to as Pangaea, and the ocean is called Panthalassa. About 140 to 180 million years ago, Pangaea began to break up into separate continents. By approximately 80 million years ago, the arrangement of the seven continents was about the same as it is today. However, the earth is always changing, and it is possible that our continents and oceans could look very different in another 80 million years.

Coasts, Shelves, and Plain

The coastlines of the oceans are always changing due to the action of waves. Waves can erode rocks and sand that make up a beach. They can reshape a beach or wear away a rocky cliff gradually over time. Reshaping can also happen quickly, due to a powerful storm such as a tsunami.

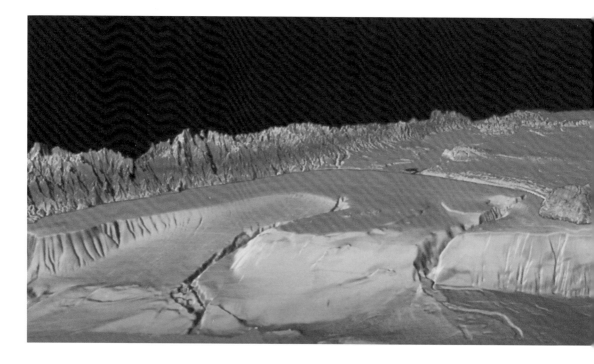

There are three types of coastline: sandy, rocky, and muddy. Sandy and rocky coasts are the most common. Muddy coastlines exist in protected areas where waves don't deposit as much rocky or sandy sediment.

The underwater areas where the oceans border land are called the continental margins. The continental margins are made up of three areas. Closest to shore is the continental shelf. The shelf is made up of the shallow water where the ocean touches the land. We know quite a bit about the continental shelf because the shallower water is easier for us to explore. Most sea life is found in the continental shelf area.

The second area of the continental margin is called the continental slope. This area has a steep drop-off just beyond the shelf. Even farther out is the third area, the continental rise. The drop-off here is not as steep, but it slopes down to a flatter area called the abyssal plain.

The abyssal plain is the deepest part of the ocean. The word "plain" is usually used to describe a large, flat area, but the abyssal

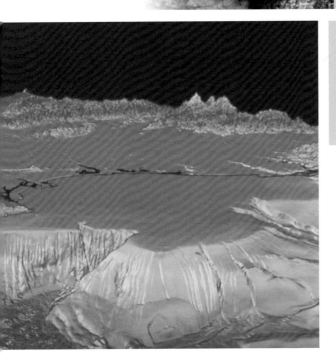

This three-dimensional model of the sea floor off the coast of Los Angeles, California, shows the shallow area of the continental shelf in pale green.

plain is not necessarily flat. In fact, there are extremely deep canyons and immensely tall volcanic mountains in the abyssal plain.

On land, the average height above sea level is 2,760 feet (840 m). The ocean is, on average, six times deeper than that. And, in some places on the ocean floor, there are canyons that are many times deeper than any canyons on land. For example, the Grand Canyon in Arizona is 5,300 feet (1,615 m) deep. In an area called the Challenger Deep in the Pacific Ocean near Guam is the undersea canyon the Mariana Trench. It is 16,400 feet (5,000 m) deeper than the ocean floor around it, and it is 35,840 feet (10,912 m) below the surface of the ocean.

In the abyssal plain, there are also several types of volcanic mountains. Some of the volcanoes rise up out of the ocean and form volcanic islands. For example, the main island of Hawaii is not only a volcanic island but is also the world's tallest mountain. It is 33,476 feet (10,203 m) from its base on the ocean floor to its highest peak.

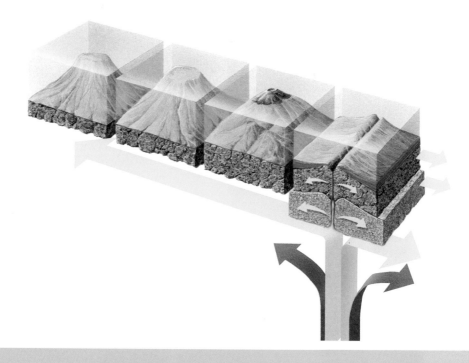

This illustration, from right to left, shows how volcanic mountains form when magma rises up from the seafloor.

Some volcanic mountains do not rise above the surface. They are called seamounts. Some seamounts, called guyots, have flat tops. Guyots used to be volcanic islands, but they eventually became covered by water.

The earth's core, which is made up of molten rock, sometimes erupts from these underwater volcanoes. The substance that comes out of a volcano is called magma. The ocean water cools the magma, forming new land. This volcanic activity keeps the earth constantly moving and changing. However, this movement is very slow, happening over thousands and thousands of years.

CHAPTER 2

THE NONLIVING ENVIRONMENT OF THE OCEANS

The five oceans contain 97.2 percent of all the water that is on the earth. Only 2.8 percent of the rest of the water on the earth is freshwater. Just a small fraction of the earth's water can be found in the thousands of lakes, ponds, reservoirs, rivers, streams, and marshes.

The water in the oceans is mostly plain water (96.5 percent). But the other 3.5 percent is chemical substances. Most of that is sodium and chloride—basic salt, such as what we use to season food.

Other substances in seawater include calcium, magnesium, potassium, and sulfur. Some of the salt in the oceans dissolved in the water from the floor of the oceans when they first formed. Other salt washes into the ocean from land.

The amount of salt in seawater varies a bit. Around the equator, where the water is warmest, seawater has the highest salt content. This is because more water evaporates in higher temperatures. This leaves more salt in the water that remains. Near the North Pole and South Pole, where the water is colder, there is less salt. There is also less salt in ocean water that is near the mouth of a river. The freshwater of the river runs into the ocean, mixing with the seawater.

Temperature

These Manganese nodules exist deep on the seabed of the Pacific Ocean.

Ocean water near the equator is the warmest. There, the sunlight hits the surface of the water most directly, and the water is above 77 degrees Fahrenheit (25 degrees Celsius). Just north and south of the equator, the water is between 50 and 77° F (10 and 25° C). Around both poles, the water temperature is between 28.7 and 50° F (-1.9 and 10° C).

Unlike freshwater, which freezes at 32° F (0° C), ocean water freezes at 28.7° F (-1.9° C). This is because the chemical substances in the water interfere with the molecules in water that bond together to form ice.

On land, the air temperature often changes a lot during just one day (between day and night, for example). In the ocean, temperatures are much steadier. Water is much slower to heat up or cool down than air. There is not much difference in temperature from day to night, or from winter to summer.

The top layer of ocean water is warmest. Beyond that, at about 985 feet (300 m), the water becomes colder. At the bottom of the ocean, temperatures are about 30 to 41° F (-1 to 5° C). This is true whether you are at the equator or at one of the poles.

Movement

Seawater is always moving, even if the surface looks smooth. There are three types of ocean movement: waves, currents, and tides.

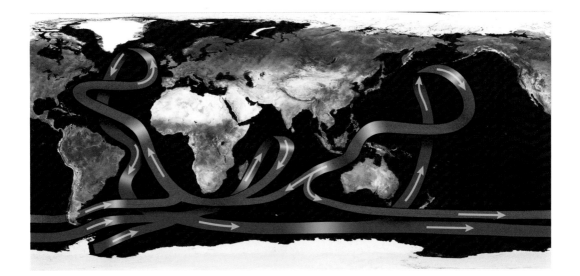

Satellite images of the earth show ocean currents. Warm water currents are shown in red; cold water currents are represented by blue.

Most waves are caused by wind. However, earthquakes or underwater volcanic eruptions can create waves that are both sudden and enormous.

Currents are large amounts of water that move in the same direction. Ocean currents are mostly the result of wind dragging the surface of the water in one direction. But some currents are due to temperature differences in the ocean. Colder water is heavier, so it sinks under warmer water, causing movement. The movement of the ocean due to currents is usually not very fast, so it is not visible on the surface. However, over time, the result of currents can be seen. For example, a boat will drift on a current, even if there is no wind.

Another kind of movement is tides. Tides are caused by the moon "pulling" the water on the earth by gravitational force. The pulling causes the water to bulge on one side, toward the moon. The water retreats on the opposite side of the earth. Because the

THE WATER CYCLE

Although the water in the oceans contains salt, oceans also create the freshwater found in lakes and other bodies of water. As water evaporates from oceans, it forms clouds. The moisture in clouds falls as rain. About 90 percent of water that evaporates from oceans falls back into the ocean as rain. The other 10 percent falls over land. This replenishes rivers, ponds, lakes, and reservoirs. This water eventually makes its way back into the ocean as rivers and streams flow back into the ocean. This process keeps the total volume of ocean water steady.

earth spins throughout the day, twice a day a particular area is in the side that's bulging. This is called high tide. Two times a day, it is directly opposite—this is low tide. In between those times, the water is headed in one or the other direction.

Light and Color in the Ocean

There are three different light zones in the ocean. In the top zone, called the sunlit zone, there is enough sunlight to allow plants to live and grow. This is the top 660 feet (200 m) of the ocean. Here, there is the most animal life because there are plants (and other animals) to feed on.

Below the sunlit zone is the twilight zone. Some sun reaches this zone but not enough for plants to survive. This zone stretches from about 660 feet to 3,300 feet (200 m to 1,000 m). Some animals spend part of their time in the twilight zone, but they swim up to the sunlit zone to feed. Other animals spend all or most of the time in the twilight zone. These animals feed on dead animals and plants that drift down from the sunlit zone.

In the sunlit zone, plants such as the kelp pictured here provide food and hiding places for thousands of varieties of fish and other sea life.

It is completely dark below the twilight zone. The midnight zone lies below 3,300 feet (1,000 m). There are very few types of animals in this zone. All of them are adapted to life in this deep, dark area.

Sunlight is made up of the colors of the rainbow. However, green and blue are the colors that travel farthest in water. This is why ocean water is usually a shade of green or blue. Blue light is the only light to reach the very bottom of the sunlit zone and the very top of the twilight zone.

CHAPTER 3

THE LIVING ENVIRONMENT OF THE OCEANS

There is an amazing amount of plant and animal life in the world's oceans. In fact, there are one thousand times more living things in the ocean than there are on land.

The smallest and most plentiful organisms in the ocean are called plankton. Ninety percent of ocean organisms are plankton. *Plankton* is the Greek word for "wanderer" or "drifter." That is just what plankton do—they drift through the ocean.

There are two types of plankton: phytoplankton and zooplankton. Phytoplankton are tiny plants. They are so small that there are millions of them in one cup of ocean water. Most are only a single cell. Because they rely on light to grow, they are found only in the sunlit zone. Zooplankton are microscopic animals. They are just as tiny as phytoplankton. They feed on phytoplankton, so they live in the sunlit zone as well. Other animals feed on zooplankton. For example, blue whales eat krill, a type of zooplankton so tiny that these whales must eat 8,000 pounds (3,629 kilograms) of them every day.

Plant Life

Besides phytoplankton, the other type of plant life in the ocean is seaweed, or kelp. Just like phytoplankton, seaweed gets its energy ("food") from sunlight. Instead of floating like phytoplankton, though, seaweed attaches to the ocean bottom. Seaweed has holdfasts (similar to roots in land plants) that anchor it to the ocean floor.

There are many types of seaweed. It can be red, green, or brown. Seaweed grows very quickly. Some types can grow 20 inches (50 centimeters) in just one day. Seaweed can also grow very tall. Some types reach heights of more than 130 feet (35 m).

Sometimes phytoplankton become so abundant they can be seen from space.

Thousands of Ocean Animals

Oceans are full of animals, from tiny crabs to enormous whales. Some of the simplest ocean animals are sponges. They gather food by slowly shifting their body parts to create movement in the water around them. They then filter the food and oxygen that they need from the water. Other simple animals include sea worms and coral.

Mollusks are a large group of animals that vary greatly in size and appearance. They range from small snails to giant squid. Most mollusks have shells covering their body, although sometimes the shells are inside the body. They usually have a strong foot, or, in the case of squid, strong feet.

Another large group of animals are arthropods. About 80 percent of the species on the earth are arthropods. Most arthropods live on land, but some make their home in the ocean, including horseshoe crabs, lobster, shrimp, and sea spiders. All arthropods have legs with joints and bodies that are covered with a hard, shell-like substance.

The giant squid is the largest invertebrate in the world. Scientists believe giant squid can grow to lengths of 65 feet (20 m), but because they live deep in the ocean, we know little about this animal.

Echinoderms are found only in the ocean. Starfish, sea urchins, sea cucumbers, and sand dollars are examples of echinoderms. Most have spines covering their body. Many echinoderms can regrow body parts if they are cut off or damaged.

All of the animals that we have discussed so far are invertebrates. This means that they have no backbone. The rest of the animals described in this section do have a backbone. They are called vertebrates.

A very large group of ocean animals are fish. An animal is considered a fish if it has a backbone and gills. Some fish have

The Living Environment of the Oceans

a skeleton that is made of cartilage, which is a hard but flexible substance. Included in this group are sharks and rays. Other fish—tuna, for example—are called bony fish because their skeletons are made of bone.

Fish come in all shapes and sizes. The whale shark is the largest fish. It weighs up to 15 tons (13.5 metric tons) and can reach 40 feet (12 m) long. Although many sharks are meat eaters, the whale shark eats only plankton.

Dolphins are highly intelligent marine mammals. They are very social, usually living in groups of about twelve.

Some mammals live on land, but there is also a large group of marine mammals. This group includes whales, dolphins, manatees, seals, sea otters, polar bears, and walruses. Mammals must breath air, so even though they can spend up to an hour underwater, they must come to the surface to breathe.

There are some reptiles that live in the ocean or split their time between land and sea. Seven kinds of turtles live in the ocean, although all lay their eggs on land. About sixty types of snakes spend some time in seawater. Two types of crocodile and one type of lizard—the marine iguana—live primarily in the ocean.

Of the 9,000 species of birds, about 350 species are considered seabirds. Although they don't spend all of their time in the water, they depend on the ocean for food, and for rest when migrating. These birds have adapted to saltwater and have webbed feet for swimming. Many types of gulls, as well as pelicans and penguins, are seabirds.

The Ocean Food Chain

The plants and animals that live in the ocean are linked together in what is called a food chain. Plants convert energy from the sun and carbon dioxide gas from the water to make their own food. Plants are called primary producers because they are the first link in the food chain. In the ocean, phytoplankton are the main primary producers.

The next link in the food chain is small organisms, such as zooplankton. These small organisms get their energy from eating plants or other small organisms. Because they eat other things, they are called primary consumers.

Animals that get their energy from eating primary consumers are called secondary consumers. Fish that eat zooplankton would be considered secondary consumers. Fish that eat other fish are the next link in the chain, called tertiary consumers. Other animals in the food chain get their energy by eating dead plants and animals.

Within a biome, several food chains may be linked where animals or plants overlap. This is called a food web. A coral reef is an example of a food web. Coral reefs are found in warm water around the world. Because coral depends on sunlight to grow, reefs are found in shallow water, mostly along coastlines.

Coral is both plant and animal. Animals called polyps make coral by absorbing calcium carbonate (a mineral in seawater). They use it to create a hard covering. Polyps then bond together, forming larger and larger coral structures. Polyps are stuck in one place but get food in two ways. During the day, phytoplankton that live in the polyps make food from sunlight. Polyps feed on the phytoplankton.

These star polyps are a type of coral. The Great Barrier Reef, the world's largest coral reef, is off the northeast coast of Australia. It covers 1,250 miles (2,000 km).

In addition, at night the polyps gather zooplankton from the water with tiny tentacles.

The phytoplankton that live in the coral are the primary producers of the coral reef food web. Phytoplankton also float in the water and live inside of other animals, such as clams. Other plants found in the coral reef are sea grass and kelp. These plants provide energy for the primary consumers, such as microscopic zooplankton. Worms, shrimp, sponges, coral polyps, and many other types of small animals eat the zooplankton. They are secondary consumers. Tertiary consumers might be fish, sharks, or eels that make their homes in and around the reef.

Sometimes, an animal can play more than one role in the food web. For example, some types of fish eat algae, so they are primary consumers. But they might also eat other fish, so they are also considered tertiary consumers.

Animal Adaptations and Behavior

All animals and plants must adapt in order to live in a particular environment. The ocean environment poses some unique challenges. But over thousands of years, animals have made adaptations that allow them to live successfully in the ocean biome.

One of the obvious challenges that ocean animals face is breathing underwater. Ocean animals need oxygen in order to live. Like mammals on land, marine mammals must breathe oxygen from the air. So, they have to rise to the surface to breathe. However, their lungs are well adapted for this and can therefore hold lots of air. Most marine mammals can stay underwater for as long as thirty minutes. Many types of whales can go without breathing for even longer; in some cases, more than one hour.

Unlike marine mammals, fish do not need to breathe air. Instead, they are able to "breathe" oxygen from water. (Water does contain oxygen, but less than air.) As fish swim through the water, slits on the sides of their bodies open to allow water to flow through. These slits are called gills. As water enters the gills, oxygen is absorbed by the fish's blood.

The bodies of most fish are uniquely adapted to life in the water. Most fish have bodies that are thin. Some are thin side to side, or flat like a ray. This shape allows them to cut through water without being slowed down by limbs. This is particularly helpful because water is denser than air, so it is more difficult to move through it quickly. Speed is especially important to some fish that must be able to evade predators. Swordfish can swim as fast as 60 miles per hour (96 kilometers per hour).

Another adaptation that helps fish swim faster is their powerful, elongated muscles. These muscles run the length of their bodies. This allows them to move their tail fins quickly, powering them through the water.

Fish move not only straight through the water, but they can also move up and down. Some fish have a swim bladder, similar to a balloon. These fish can add more air to the swim bladder when they want to go closer to the surface of the water. To sink, they let air out of the swim bladder.

Water temperature in oceans stays about the same year round in a particular location. So, ocean plants and animals do not need to adapt to the change in seasons like living things on land must. However, some animals must adapt to a particularly harsh environment. Animals that live in the extremely cold water in the polar regions have large stores of fat to help keep them warm. Others, such as polar bears, have thick fur for warmth.

This barbeled dragonfish has adapted to the darkness of the deep ocean by using a bioluminescent lure on its chin to attract prey.

Animals that live in the ocean depths (the midnight zone) have to make many adaptations. Because it is completely dark in the midnight zone, these animals have a good sense of smell in order to find food. There is not much food to go around because so few fish live in this zone. When they find a meal, they must eat all they can. For this reason, their mouths and stomachs are large. Sometimes, a large carcass (a whale, for example) lands on the ocean floor. The fish in this zone can feed on it for months. Some animals in the midnight zone are able to create a type of light called bioluminescence. The light attracts prey.

CHAPTER 4

GLOBAL WARMING AND ITS EFFECTS ON THE OCEANS

Many elements work together to keep the earth's climate in balance. The sun, ocean, wind, land, and atmosphere all play a role. For the climate to stay the same, there can't be large changes to any part of the system. Over the past thirty years, scientists have begun to notice significant changes in our climate system. Evidence suggests that the earth's climate is warming.

The Climate in Balance

The oceans are a very important part of the earth's climate system. Water stores heat well because it does not get hotter or colder as quickly as the air does. Water also helps distribute heat around the planet by way of the oceans' currents, keeping air temperature steady. Ice in the oceans also plays a role in keeping the climate in balance. Icebergs near the poles and ice covering Antarctica and Greenland reflect the sun's rays back into the atmosphere. This prevents the air near the surface of the earth from getting too warm.

It is normal for the climate to change slowly over time. Usually, these changes are gradual and happen in cycles. Although the earth may warm over a period of years or

If these icebergs off the coast of Antarctica melt, they will not cause a rise in sea level. Of more concern is melting glaciers, which will add water to the world's oceans.

decades, it eventually cools again. This is a natural process. However, in the late 1970s, scientists began to notice that there were some potentially unnatural climate changes occurring. They suspected that humans might have something to do with these changes.

In the 1980s, scientists began to look closely at the possibility of climate change. They studied fossils, soil samples, ice samples, and other evidence to see if they could separate natural climate change cycles from changes brought about by humans. The results of their studies seemed to indicate that the earth's climate was warming. Although not all scientists agreed, the results also suggested that humans have played a role.

THE GREENHOUSE EFFECT

One major way that humans might be contributing to the warming of the earth is through what is called the greenhouse effect. As part of the normal climate system, some of the sun's energy is absorbed by the earth's atmosphere. The rest of this energy hits the surface of the earth—land and oceans. Some of the heat energy is absorbed by the surface, and some of it is reflected back into the atmosphere.

Some gases, such as carbon dioxide and methane, build up in the atmosphere. These gases trap heat energy from the sun, and this warms both the atmosphere and the earth's surface. Although these gases are normally present in the atmosphere, humans are adding large amounts through the use of cars, power plants, and other activities. Cutting down forests also plays a role because trees remove carbon dioxide from the air. With fewer trees on the planet, less carbon dioxide is removed from the atmosphere.

The surface of the earth reflects about 30 percent of the sun's energy back into space, and about 70 percent remains trapped in the atmosphere.

There were twenty-eight major storms in the Atlantic in 2005, the most on record. The 2005 hurricane season included Hurricane Wilma, pictured here, and Hurricane Katrina, which caused more than 1,800 deaths.

Effects of Global Warming

Global warming can potentially cause many problems for humans and the environment. For example, warmer air temperatures may cause more and longer heat waves. These can cause human and animal deaths and droughts.

Scientists have found that the top 1,000 feet (300 m) of oceans have gotten .67° F (.31° C) warmer in the last fifty years. This may not seem like a lot, but it is having several effects. Warmer ocean temperatures have melted glaciers, adding to the overall amount of water in oceans. Higher temperatures also cause water to expand, adding to the overall volume of water. These things have caused the sea level to rise. This can cause worse flooding during storms, and it may lead to loss of land along shorelines if the sea level continues to rise.

Warmer ocean temperatures may cause weather problems. More extreme weather, such as more frequent and stronger hurricanes, may occur. If oceans are warmer, then they evaporate more quickly. This can cause changes in weather patterns. There may be more rainfall in some places and drought in other places.

Rising temperatures can also affect plant and animal habitats. Coral reefs suffer due to several effects of global warming. The increase in the amount of carbon dioxide in the environment increases the acidity of seawater. This makes it harder for the coral to grow. Higher water temperatures also stress the coral and kill the algae that live in the coral. This is called bleaching. Without coral reefs, some species of ocean animals could become extinct. Animals in polar habitats are affected as well. For example, due to melting glaciers, polar bears have less room to roam and hunt for food.

CHAPTER 5

THE FUTURE OF THE OCEANS

Unfortunately, global warming is not the only problem for the world's oceans. Pollution, overfishing, and damage from ships are just some of the threats to the health of the oceans.

Many pollutants enter the oceans from rivers and streams that empty into them. Salt that is used to treat icy roads, garbage, and sewage can all wash into the ocean from sewers. Pesticides used on farm fields can enter the freshwater supply and eventually the ocean. These chemicals can damage or kill sea life.

Some pollutants kill ocean plants and animals immediately. Others cause problems by building up in the bodies of animals. These pollutants are absorbed by phytoplankton or zooplankton. The chemicals build up in their cells. When other animals eat the plankton, their bodies absorb the pollutants in concentrated form. This process continues all the way up the food chain. At the end of the food chain, a toxic chemical is so concentrated that it can be at a level one million times higher than it was originally. Polar bears are especially susceptible to this problem for two reasons. One is that many chemicals drift into Arctic waters on ocean currents. The other reason is that chemicals break down more slowly in the cold water of their habitat.

Fertilizers used in farming can end up in the ocean, too. You might think that fertilizer would be a good thing, but it can lead

Chemicals such as fertilizer can lead to excess algae (called a bloom). Dead algae can create this foamy scum along beaches.

to too much algae in the ocean. With extra algae, more animals can feed. But eventually, there are more dead plants and animals. The organisms that feed on the decomposing plants and animals use up oxygen in the water, which can kill fish and plants. This creates what are called dead zones, where nothing can live. Sometimes, a dead zone is temporary and eventually there is enough oxygen to again support plants and animals. There are some permanent dead zones though, including one in the Baltic Sea.

Another threat is excess soil washing into the ocean. In places where entire forests are cut down for lumber or to make way for houses, there are no longer enough tree roots and other plants to hold the soil together. When it rains, the loose soil enters the rivers and streams. It washes into the ocean, clogging the water. This can affect the oxygen content of water.

Threats from the Sea

Several major threats to the oceans come from the fishing industry. One problem is overfishing. Technology has made us better at fishing. However, we have become so good at fishing that we are killing too many fish. This can use up not only the species being fished but also the other species that depend on that type of fish. As a result, food webs are disturbed.

Another hazard is that some fishing methods harm other, unintended fish. These fish and other animals are called bycatch. They get caught in fishing nets and are usually killed. Nineteen million pounds (8.6 million kg) of bycatch each year are killed just by the people fishing for shrimp.

Other fishing methods harm the ocean floor, disturbing or killing the animals that live on the bottom. Still other fishing practices use cyanide or dynamite to stun fish. These methods also poison or kill unintended fish and destroy coral reefs.

Overfishing and pollution are serious threats to the ocean's fish populations. A 2006 report in *Science* magazine suggests that by the year 2048, there may no longer be enough fish for humans to eat.

Fishing nets that are lost or thrown away are another potential danger. They can trap seals, turtles, or birds and cause them to drown or choke to death.

Other threats come from boats. Oil spills or garbage dumped from ships cause many problems for ocean life. Plastic bags are especially harmful when swallowed by fish or turtles that mistake them for food. Boats can also destroy coral reefs.

An additional problem facing the world's oceans is "alien," or invasive, species. Occasionally, a species of fish enters a new habitat by mistake. For example, large ships sometimes travel with water in the bottom of the ship for balance. When the ships reach their destinations and the water is dumped, any fish that are still alive enter the habitat. With no natural predators in this new environment, the population of the "alien" fish can get out of control. This can upset the balance of the food web, too.

What Can We Do to Protect the Future of the Oceans?

Although the problems facing the world's oceans are large and there are many of them, there are still things that can be done to help. Many of the solutions require the participation of all the countries around the world. This is because there are no borders in the ocean. Pollution in one area simply drifts to a new area on the ocean's currents.

There are several global groups that are working to solve the ocean's problems. One major group is the Intergovernmental Panel on Climate Change (IPCC). It is studying the effects of global warming and is creating plans to help off-set its effects. Along with former U.S. vice president Al Gore, the IPCC won a Nobel Peace Prize in 2007 for its work. The Global Ocean Observing System (GOOS) is also studying the effects of global warming. It focuses on the oceans in particular.

In addition to trying to fight global warming's effects on the oceans, we must also try to fix

The U.S. Navy ship *Spiegel Grove* was intentionally sunk off Key Largo, Florida, to create an artificial coral reef.

problems faced by ocean plants and animals. Setting limits on the amount of fish that the fishing industry can catch could help. Creating protected areas where fishing is banned is another solution. This can allow the fish population to increase.

To offset the damage being done to coral reefs, we can create new ones. In several places around the world, old ships have intentionally been sunk in shallow water so that new coral reefs will grow on the ships. Within a few months, creatures like anemones and barnacles attach to these ships and other animals eventually begin to live in and around the reef.

Governments or other large organizations must implement the solutions mentioned so far. What can individuals do to help? To fight global warming, do everything you can to use less energy from fossil fuels. Organize carpools or ride your bike to school or activities. Buy energy-efficient light bulbs and appliances. Turn off lights when you are not in the room and computers when you are not using them. Recycle, or avoid buying items that you don't need.

Stay informed about things that you can do to help the oceans. Get involved with groups working to change energy practices or researching solutions to the ocean's problems. If you eat fish, then find out how the fish are caught to be sure they are caught by using responsible practices.

Study oceanography or marine biology, or consider a career in one of the many fields relating to the ocean. Maybe you will be one of the people who find a solution to the many problems facing our oceans.

acidity The amount of acid dissolved in another substance.

climate The average weather in a region.

comet An object from space made up of ice and dust.

coniferous forest A forest made up of evergreen (pine) trees.

core The center of the earth.

cyanide A poison that can stun or kill fish.

elongated Long; stretched out.

equator The imaginary line around the earth, dividing it between north and south.

evade To escape or avoid.

evaporate To turn from liquid into vapor.

fossil The remains of an ancient plant or animal preserved in rock or soil.

geographer A scientist who studies the location of living and nonliving things.

molecule The smallest particle of a substance that still has all the properties of that substance.

organism A living person, animal, or plant.

pollutant Something that contaminates water, soil, or air.

replenish To fill up again.

reservoir A natural or artificial lake where water is collected and stored.

terrestrial Of or related to land; things that live or grow on land.

tsunami A huge wave created by an underwater eruption of a volcano or an earthquake.

zone A region or area.

Conservation International

201 Crystal Drive, Suite 500

Arlington, VA 22202

(800) 429-5660

Web site: http://www.conservation.org

This organization seeks to "conserve Earth's living heritage, our global biodiversity, and to demonstrate that human societies are able to live harmoniously with nature."

Cousteau Society

710 Settlers Landing Road

Hampton, VA 23669

(800) 441-4395

Web site: http://www.cousteau.org

The Cousteau Society is dedicated to protecting oceans and marine life. It has a bimonthly magazine for kids, *Cousteau Kids*, and resources for teachers.

Earth Force

2120 West 33rd Avenue

Denver, CO 80211

(303) 482-2139

Web site: http://www.earthforce.org

Earth Force is an organization that works to involve kids in environmental causes. It runs programs in several cities around the United States and provides tools for teachers.

Fisheries and Oceans Canada

200 Kent Street

13th Floor, Station 13228

Ottawa, ON K1A 0E6
Canada
(613) 993-0999
Web site: http://www.dfo-mpo.gc.ca/home-accueil_e.htm
This branch of the Canadian government is in charge of protecting
   the marine environment in Canada.

Greenpeace
702 H Street NW, Suite 300
Washington, DC 20001
(800) 326-0959
Web site: http://www.greenpeace.org/usa/campaigns/oceans
Greenpeace has been working to protect the world's oceans and
   marine life since 1971.

National Aquarium in Baltimore
501 East Pratt Street
Baltimore, MD 21202
(410) 576-3800
Web site: http://www.aqua.org/index.html
Visit the National Aquarium or its Web site for information on sea
   creatures, oceans, and conservation.

National Oceanic and Atmospheric Administration (NOAA)
1401 Constitution Avenue NW, Room 6217
Washington, DC 20230
(202) 482-6090
Web site: http://www.noaa.gov
NOAA is a U.S. government agency that monitors weather, climate,
   and all aspects of the marine environment.

Ocean Conservancy

1300 19th Street NW, 8th Floor

Washington, DC 20036

(800) 519-1541

Web site: http://www.oceanconservancy.org

Ocean Conservancy "promotes healthy and diverse ocean ecosystems and opposes practices that threaten ocean life and human life."

World Wildlife Fund-Canada

245 Eglinton Avenue East, Suite 410

Toronto, ON M4P 3J1

Canada

(800) 26-PANDA (267-2632)

Web site: http://www.wwf.ca

WWF-Canada is a branch of the World Wildlife Fund, which works to conserve and protect land, oceans, and wildlife.

Web Sites

Due to the changing nature of Internet links, Rosen Publishing has developed an online list of Web sites related to the subject of this book. This site is updated regularly. Please use this link to access the list:

http://www.rosenlinks.com/biom/ocea

FOR FURTHER READING

Brezina, Corona. *Climate Change*. New York, NY: Rosen Publishing, 2008.

The Diagram Group. *Marine Science: An Illustrated Guide to Science*. New York, NY: Chelsea House Publishers, 2006.

Donovan, Sandra. *Ocean Animals*. Austin, TX: Steadwell Books, 2002.

Earle, Sylvia A. *Dive! Adventures in the Deep Frontier*. Washington, DC: National Geographic Society, 1999.

Gore, Al. *An Inconvenient Truth: The Crisis of Global Warming*. Adapted for young readers by Jane O'Connor. New York, NY: Viking, 2007.

Johansson, Philip. *The Coral Reef: A Colorful Web of Life*. Berkeley Heights, NJ: Enslow Publishers, Inc., 2008.

Johansson, Philip. *The Seashore: A Saltwater Web of Life*. Berkeley Heights, NJ: Enslow Publishers, Inc., 2008.

Lambert, David. *The Kingfisher Young People's Book of Oceans*. New York, NY: Kingfisher, 1997.

McMillan, Beverly, and John A. Musick. *Oceans*. New York, NY: Simon & Schuster Books for Young Readers, 2007.

Nye, Bill, with Ian G. Saunders. *Bill Nye the Science Guy's Big Blue Ocean*. New York, NY: Hyperion Books for Children, 1999.

Day, Trevor. *Oceans*. Revised ed. New York, NY: Facts On File, Inc., 2008.

The Diagram Group. *Marine Science: An Illustrated Guide to Science*. New York, NY: Chelsea House Publishers, 2006.

DiMento, Joseph F. C., and Pamela Doughman. *Climate Change: What It Means to Us, Our Children, and Our Grandchildren*. Cambridge, MA: The MIT Press, 2007.

Handwerk, Brian. "Tsunami Redraws Indian Ocean Maps." *National Geographic*, January 12, 2005.

Hoffman, Jennifer. *Science 101: Ocean Science*. New York, NY: HarperCollins Publishers, 2007.

Intergovernmental Panel on Climate Change. *Climate Change 2007: The Physical Science Basis*. February 2007. Retrieved February 14, 2008 (http://www.ipcc.ch/ipccreports/ ar4-wg1.htm).

Kalman, Bobbie. *What Is a Biome?* New York, NY: Crabtree Publishing, 1998.

McMillan, Beverly, and John A. Musick. *Oceans*. New York, NY: Simon & Schuster Books for Young Readers, 2007.

Nye, Bill, with Ian G. Saunders. *Bill Nye the Science Guy's Big Blue Ocean*. New York, NY: Hyperion Books for Children, 1999.

Ricciuti, Edward R. *Biomes of the World: Ocean*. New York, NY: Benchmark Books, 1996.

West, Krista, ed. *Critical Perspectives on the Oceans*. New York, NY: Rosen Publishing, 2007.

Woodward, Susan L. *Biomes of Earth: Terrestrial, Aquatic, and Human-Dominated*. Westport, CT: Greenwood Press, 2003.

INDEX

A

abyssal plains, 12–13
algae, 26, 33, 36
Antarctic Ocean, 7, 9
Arctic Ocean, 7, 9
arthropods, 21
Atlantic Ocean, 7, 9

B

bioluminescence, 28
biomes, divisions of, 5–6
bleaching, 33
bycatch, 36

C

cartilage, 22–23
coastlines, types of, 12
continental crust, 11
continental margins, areas of, 12
coral reefs, 24–25, 33, 36–37, 39

D

dead zones, 36
dolphins, 23

E

echinoderms, 22

F

fish population, 23, 26–28, 36–39
food webs, 24, 36
freshwater, 6, 15–16, 18

G

geographers, 7
Global Ocean Observing System (GOOS), 38
global warming, 29–31, 33, 34, 38–39
Gore, Al, 38
greenhouse effect, 31
guyots, 14

I

Indian Ocean, 7, 9
Intergovernmental Panel on Climate Change (IPCC), 38
invertebrates, 22

K

kelp, 20, 25

L

light zones, ocean, 18

M

magma, 14
manatees, 23
marine biology, 39
midnight zone, 19, 28
mollusks, 21

O

oceanic crust, 11
oceanography, 39

About the Author

Simone Payment has a degree in psychology from Cornell University and a master's degree in elementary education from Wheelock College. She is the author of nineteen books for young adults. Her book *Inside Special Operations: Navy SEALs* (also from Rosen Publishing) won a 2004 Quick Picks for Reluctant Young Readers award from the American Library Association and is on the Nonfiction Honor List of Voice of Youth Advocates. The ocean is one of her favorite places to visit and study.

Photo Credits

Cover, back cover, pp. 7, 15, 20, 29, 34 © www.istockphoto.com/Terraxplorer; cover (inset), pp. 1, 7, 15, 20, 29, 34 © www.istockphoto.com/John Anderson; pp. 4–5, 19, 23, 25, 30, 35 Shutterstock.com; pp. 8, 9 courtesy of the University of Texas Libraries, the University of Texas at Austin; p. 10 © John Baumgardner, LANL/Photo Researchers, Inc.; pp. 12–13 USGS/Photo Researchers, Inc.; pp. 14, 31 © Gary Hinks/Photo Researchers, Inc.; p. 16 © Peter Ryan/Photo Researchers, Inc.; p. 17 © SPL/Photo Researchers, Inc.; p. 21 HO/AFP/Getty Images; p. 22 © Christian Darkin/Photo Researchers, Inc.; p. 27 © Dante Fenolio/Photo Researchers, Inc.; p. 32 NOAA via Getty Images; p. 37 Marcel Mochet/AFP/Getty Images; p. 38 Bob Care/AFP/Getty Images; back cover inset images (left to right) © www.istockphoto.com/Lilli Day, © www.istockphoto.com/Maceofoto, © www.istockphoto.com/David Gunn, © www.istockphoto.com/Paul Senyszyn, © www.istockphoto.com/John Anderson, © www.istockphoto.com/TT.

Designer: Les Kanturek; Editor: Nicholas Croce
Photo Researcher: Cindy Reiman